Swim
Workouts

FOR TRIATHLETES

PRACTICAL WORKOUTS TO BUILD SPEED, STRENGTH, AND ENDURANCE

2ND EDITION

GALE BERNHARDT & NICK HANSEN

Boulder, Colorado

1830 55th Street
Boulder, Colorado 80301-2700 USA
(303) 440-0601 · Fax (303) 444-6788 · E-mail velopress@competitorgroup.com

Distributed in the United States and Canada by Ingram Publisher Services

Library of Congress Cataloging-in-Publication Data
Bernhardt, Gale, 1958–
Swim workouts for triathletes: practical workouts to build speed, strength, and endurance / Gale Bernhardt and Nick Hansen.—2nd ed.
        p. cm.
ISBN 978-1-934030-75-2 (spiral-bound: alk. paper)
1. Swimming—Training. 2. Triathlon—Training. I. Hansen, Nick. II. Title.
GV837.7.B37 2011
797.2'1—dc22
        2010053058

For information on purchasing VeloPress books, please call (800) 811-4210 ext. 2169 or visit www.velopress.com.

Cover design by theBookDesigners
Cover photograph by Delly Carr
Interior design by Jessica Xavier
Interior illustrations by Charlie Layton

Text set in Dante and Gotham Narrow.

11 12 13 / 10 9 8 7 6 5 4 3 2 1

Contents

Workouts   33

Acknowledgments

Special thanks go to Amy McGrath, Alexander Durst, and Dallas Schoo for providing feedback on workouts. The second edition of this book was greatly improved by Charlie Layton's excellent illustrations. Connie Oehring, Jessica Xavier, and Renee Jardine brought the product to life with their editorial and creative improvements, including new colors and improved readability.

Introduction

For many triathletes, swimming is a real challenge. It's typically the sport in which they have least experience, least efficiency, and plenty of room for improvement. *Swim Workouts for Triathletes* is the perfect tool for swimmers of all levels because it offers the variety and depth athletes need to swim faster and achieve their fitness goals.

One thing that makes swimming different from other sports, namely cycling and running, is that the training venue is usually the same—25 meters of clear water with a black line along the bottom of each lane. When you do an aerobic cycling or running workout, you probably choose from a variety of courses to eliminate boredom. For a swim, you usually can't vary the course, but if you draw from a variety of workouts, your time in the pool will be interesting and more rewarding.

These workouts can easily be used in conjunction with your current training plan or as standalone workouts. If you use Gale's triathlon training book, *Training Plans for Multisport Athletes* (VeloPress, 2006), you will be familiar with the terminology used here and will find the workouts to be compatible. If you are following another program, you can simply identify the workout category that best suits your goals (see "Finding the Right Workout"). If you are not currently following a training plan, we have provided four plans for you to choose from, three of which are particular to the most common race distances: sprint (0.5-mile swim), Olympic (0.8-mile swim) and half-Ironman® (1.2-mile swim), and Ironman® (2.4-mile swim). As you get a better understanding of your own strengths and weaknesses, you can design your own plan for improvement. Our 12-week general fitness training plan is a great guide to get you started. For more on the training plans, see the "Training Plans" section of this book.

Best of all, this book is completely waterproof! You can set it on the pool deck—the practical design can be easily converted to an upright display so that you can easily review your workout between sets. But before you jump in, let's take a closer look at the benefits of each different type of workout.

Finding the Right Workout

Generally, all of these swimming workouts have a warm-up set, a main set, and a cooldown set. Most of the workouts also provide two main sets to choose from: beginner or advanced. Choose the main set that is most appropriate for both your ability level and your available workout time. Plenty of experienced swimmers will opt to swim a "beginner" set when they are pressed for time. A word of caution to less experienced swimmers: You will find greater improvement through quality sets, not quantity. You might be able to push through a 3000-meter workout, but as you tire, your form can suffer, making those extra laps less than beneficial. In many cases, you will find that it's better to do three or four swims each week rather than to rack up the same distance in just two workouts.

The title of each workout indicates its primary purpose or goal. There are workouts to develop aerobic endurance, form, speed, pacing, and strength (or force) in the water. Each workout category can be matched to one of the training zones listed in Table 1. These training zones or intensities are common across most training programs. You can also identify the correct intensity using the Borg Scale, or Rating of Perceived Exertion (RPE). As you improve as a swimmer, you will be able to do more or swim faster at lower exertion levels. You'll find that RPE and regular time trials (see "Testing") provide valuable feedback on your training progress.

TABLE 1 | Training & Racing Intensities

Training Zone	Workout Type	RPE	Breathing	Purpose/Description
1	Endurance	6–9	Hardly noticeable	Aerobic, recovery
2	Endurance	10–12	Slightly strained	Aerobic, extensive endurance
3	Endurance Muscular Endurance Distance	13–14	Breathing a little harder	Tempo, intensive endurance
4	Muscular Endurance Occasional Force	15–16	Starting to breathe hard	Subthreshold, muscular endurance, threshold endurance, lactate threshold
5a	Muscular Endurance Occasional Force	17	Breathing hard	Superthreshold, muscular endurance, threshold endurance, lactate threshold
5b	Anaerobic Endurance	18–19	Heavy, labored breath	Aerobic capacity, speed endurance, anaerobic endurance, anaerobic threshold
5c	All-out, fast sprints	20	Maximal exertion/ breathing	Anaerobic capacity, power

There are nine different workout categories used in this book. First explore all of them, then focus on those that best fit your goals.

ENDURANCE (E) WORKOUTS

These workouts emphasize aerobic work. The main set is typically 20 to 40 minutes long, containing broken sets with rest intervals of 15 seconds or less. Swim at a pace that allows you to complete the entire set without taking extra rest. This speed is typically 5 to 8 seconds per 100 slower than T-pace. (We'll help you find your test pace in the "Testing" section.) You'll notice that Endurance workouts span zones 1, 2, and 3. On any given day you could choose to control the intensity of your endurance workout. If you need a recovery day, you might swim more in zones 1 and 2. If you are feeling particularly fresh, you could push to zone 3.

E Speed
The main sets of these workouts are mostly aerobic work, although the end of each workout includes some very fast 25s or 50s with an emphasis on high-speed arm turnover. Generally there is ample rest between swim sections to allow full recovery. Take more rest if you need it. During the speed set, neuromuscular training is more important than sustaining a high heart rate.

E Form
The main set is mostly aerobic work, but you'll find some form work at the beginning of the workout. Some coaches refer to this as "drill work." Like the speed sets, these are short sets, but good form is more important than speed. This type of neuromuscular training will help you learn the correct stroke mechanics so you can move more quickly and efficiently through the water.

FORCE (F) WORKOUTS
These workouts are intended to improve swimming strength, typically requiring a pull buoy for a significant portion of the main set. Using paddles with the pull buoy is optional but highly recommended. Think of it as a strength training workout in the pool. If you are just beginning to use paddles, use them for just a portion of the main set and gradually increase the distance over several workouts.

MUSCULAR ENDURANCE (ME) WORKOUTS
These workouts develop your pacing. They are often referred to as lactate threshold or anaerobic threshold workouts. It is important to be well rested as you head into a Muscular Endurance session.

The main sets are combinations of distances lasting 20 to 40 minutes. You'll swim a good portion of the main set at T-pace or 2 to 5 seconds faster. Swim intervals might be 50 to 200 meters, and depending on the length of each swim, rest intervals are 5 to 20 seconds. Make it your goal to sustain T-pace or go slightly faster.

ME Distance

The main sets of these workouts are done at half-Ironman- or Ironman-distance race pace (1.2 and 2.4 miles, respectively). Depending on your fitness, strengths, and racing limitations, this pace is typically 3 to 10 seconds slower than your 100-meter T-pace. The distance workouts do not have beginner and advanced sets. The second column will give you additional direction or strategies for successfully completing the main set.

ANAEROBIC ENDURANCE (An)

The goal of these workouts is to swim very fast—faster than you thought possible. You will achieve your best results during Anaerobic Endurance sessions if you are well rested. The main set may be quite short in distance but still take 20 to 40 minutes to complete. Your primary objective is to swim fast—don't conserve energy. You may find that your speed decreases as the set goes on. In most cases, that's okay because you simply want to achieve the fastest speed possible for that given swim. However, if you are unable to swim faster than T-pace, stop the set, swim easy, and try again another day.

30-MINUTE (30M) WORKOUTS

These workouts are intended to help you fit in a quality swim even when you are short on time. Most of the workouts involve a combination of skills and intensities. Because you are swimming for only 30 minutes, you might be able to swim harder. Depending on your pace, you might need to adjust the number of sets that you swim in order to be in and out of the pool quickly. Or you can stay to finish the workout . . . we won't tell anyone.

OPEN-WATER (OW) WORKOUTS

Most triathlons involve an open-water swim. Although you could use many of the workouts in this book in an open-water training session or race prep, we want to give you some workouts that are focused on the skills you need to keep your wits about you and stay on pace come race day. You'll practice pacing and sighting over intervals short and long. These workouts vary in duration and difficulty. As with the Muscular Endurance Distance workouts, there is only one set rather than beginner and advanced sets. Read the additional instruction and tips to find the workout that works best for your race distance or allotted time.

Testing (T)

Many of the workouts we've written specify a pace to shoot for, which we call T-pace. This pace varies from one swimmer to the next. You can find your T-pace by doing an individual time trial. The distance of your time trial will depend on your fitness or event distance. For sprint-distance triathlons, use Test A. (Beginners will also want to start with this test.) For all other event distances, use Test B.

For both tests, the goal of the main set is to swim at the fastest possible sustained speed in order to achieve the lowest average time. You will average the time for all three sets to establish your T-pace. Pacing is critical. Do not swim a fast first interval and find yourself with nothing left for the third interval. If you were doing Test A, successful pacing would be three sets of 100 meters swum at 1:25, 1:21, and 1:24—making the T-pace 1:23. If you finished that third interval in 1:35, you would have a 14-second difference from

TABLE 2 | Finding Your T-pace per 100 m

300 Average Time	T-pace per 100	300 Average Time	T-pace per 100
2:39:00	0:53:00	4:21:00	1:27:00
2:42:00	0:54:00	4:24:00	1:28:00
2:45:00	0:55:00	4:27:00	1:29:00
2:48:00	0:56:00	4:30:00	1:30:00
2:51:00	0:57:00	4:33:00	1:31:00
2:54:00	0:58:00	4:36:00	1:32:00
2:57:00	0:59:00	4:39:00	1:33:00
3:00:00	1:00:00	4:42:00	1:34:00
3:03:00	1:01:00	4:45:00	1:35:00
3:06:00	1:02:00	4:48:00	1:36:00
3:09:00	1:03:00	4:51:00	1:37:00
3:12:00	1:04:00	4:54:00	1:38:00
3:15:00	1:05:00	4:57:00	1:39:00
3:18:00	1:06:00	5:00:00	1:40:00
3:21:00	1:07:00	5:03:00	1:41:00
3:24:00	1:08:00	5:06:00	1:42:00
3:27:00	1:09:00	5:09:00	1:43:00
3:30:00	1:10:00	5:12:00	1:44:00
3:33:00	1:11:00	5:15:00	1:45:00
3:36:00	1:12:00	5:18:00	1:46:00
3:39:00	1:13:00	5:21:00	1:47:00
3:42:00	1:14:00	5:24:00	1:48:00
3:45:00	1:15:00	5:27:00	1:49:00
3:48:00	1:16:00	5:30:00	1:50:00
3:51:00	1:17:00	5:33:00	1:51:00
3:54:00	1:18:00	5:36:00	1:52:00
3:57:00	1:19:00	5:39:00	1:53:00
4:00:00	1:20:00	5:42:00	1:54:00
4:03:00	1:21:00	5:45:00	1:55:00
4:06:00	1:22:00	5:48:00	1:56:00
4:09:00	1:23:00	5:51:00	1:57:00
4:12:00	1:24:00	5:54:00	1:58:00
4:15:00	1:25:00	5:57:00	1:59:00
4:18:00	1:26:00	6:00:00	2:00:00

your fastest time. For Test A, it is best if all three 100s are within 5 seconds of one another.

Test B is a 300-meter time trial. You will want all three sets to be within 15 seconds of one another. Add up your times and divide by three to find your average time for 300 meters. Table 2 will help you quickly find your 100-meter pace, or T-pace. This particular pace is used to approximate lactate threshold pace.

Testing is typically done every three to four weeks and is best accomplished during a rest week. Some athletes prefer to test every other rest week, or every six to eight weeks. Improving T-pace over several weeks and months of training is a marker of improved fitness and certainly a goal to shoot for.

If you are just beginning to get in shape, use the RPE guidelines in Table 1 until you build enough fitness to complete the time trial. If you have special health conditions, consult a physician about any necessary restrictions on exercise intensities.

Pacing in Different Workouts

To illustrate how to use the workouts to improve swimming, let's consider an example. Michelle is training for an Olympic-distance triathlon. She completes Test B and finds her average pace for 300 meters to be 4:15. Using Table 2, she finds her T-pace (or pace per 100 meters) to be 1:25.

For Michelle to progress and swim faster, she should swim at specific paces for different workouts without compromising rest. Her pace will change depending on the goal of the workout. Table 3 illustrates how Michelle should approach different workouts based on her current T-pace of 1:25. She will periodically test herself, and as her time trials speed up, her T-pace will decrease. (For details on Michelle's test sets, see Table 3.)

TABLE 3 | Michelle's Swims

Workout Code	Description	Main Set	Pace
Tb	300-m Time Trial	3 × 300 (0:30RI) Result: 4:17, 4:15, 4:13 Average 300 time at 4:15	Resulting T1-pace at 1:25 per 100

Workout Code	Description	Sample Set	Goal Pace
E1	Endurance (Zone 1)	8 × 200	Ignore the clock, make RPE zone 1
E2	Endurance (Zone 2)	8 × 200 on a 3:20SI (swim interval)	Hold 1:30–1:35 pace per 100
E3	Endurance (Zone 3)	8 × 200 on a 3:15SI	Hold 1:25–1:30 pace per 100 or 2:50–3:00 per 200
Force	Force	5 × 200 with paddles on a 3:15SI	Hold 1:20–1:25 pace
ME	Muscular Endurance	5–6 × 200 on a 3:05SI	Hold 1:20–1:25 pace
A	Anaerobic Endurance	8 × 50 on a 2:30SI	Hold under 0:35 pace per 50

Training Plans

If you hope to improve your swimming, you must formulate a plan. Too often, triathletes mix and match workouts or parts of workouts with no particular goal in mind, and this habit tends to lead to mediocre swimming. The following four training plans offer balanced training and promise improved performance.

Each training plan allows for flexibility. You can choose which days of the week are best for your swim workouts; we have specified days of the week mainly to give you an idea of how the workouts should be timed. Once you recognize the pattern of each plan, you can add another block of training (2 or 3 weeks of volume followed by 1 week of rest) to extend a plan or to better complement your cycling and running training.

As you modify any of the plans to meet your personal needs, be conscious of the temptation to either remove too much volume or add more volume than necessary. Although athletes with a strong swimming history can achieve success with less volume, that choice may not be a good one for you. On the other hand, swimming more than necessary can rob you of the energy needed for workouts in other sports and can lead to injuries.

12-Week General Fitness Swim Plan

The first swim plan is designed to help you change gears. Some days are for recovery, taking it easy in the pool; other days provide fast workouts with no holding back. Endurance workouts build or maintain aerobic endurance. The Speed and Form workouts also work on endurance but are targeted toward a component of neuro-muscular form—for example, correct stroke mechanics or the ability to move quickly and efficiently for short distances. Muscular Endurance days work on your ability to swim a fast, steady pace for longer distances. Force workouts focus on sport strength. Anaerobic Endurance work helps you improve your speed in what swimmers call middle distances.

This 12-week plan can be used to build fitness or prepare for a race of any distance. We have left it up to you to select specific workouts, simply specifying the appropriate workout category for each day. Be deliberate in choosing workouts that challenge you and help you meet your goal.

Within each workout, choose the "beginner" or "advanced" column that allows you to complete your workout in 30 to 60 minutes and suits your current range of speed. In some cases, you may want to reduce the number of sets in a given workout to accomplish your goal. In other cases, you may want to increase the number of sets.

Enjoy the process of changing speeds and improving your pace.

General Fitness Training Plan

Week	TUESDAY	THURSDAY	FRIDAY (optional)	SATURDAY
1	T	E Form	F	E Speed
2	E	E Form	F	ME
3	E	E Speed	F	E
4	T	E Form	An	E
5	ME	E	F	An
6	ME	E	An	E Form
7	T	E	F	An
8	E Speed	ME	An	E Form
9	E	ME	T	E
10	ME	E	F	An
11	E	ME	Day off	E
12	An	E	Day off	Race

Note: Workouts may be done any day of the week. Days shown here are meant to demonstrate how best to space workouts over the course of a week.

15-Week Sprint-Distance Swim Plan

This plan will help you prepare for a shorter race or improve performance. If you are training for a sprint-distance triathlon, you don't need to swim as many meters or yards as when training for a longer-distance event. However, it is still valuable to include some longer distances in addition to fast, short intervals. The variety in your training will build fitness and ultimately make you faster.

This 15-week plan consists of two workouts per week for 2 weeks, followed by a recovery week during which you swim just once. The plan slots in weekly workouts on Tuesdays and Thursdays; however, you can move the workouts to the days of the week that work best for you. Try to separate swim workouts by 48 hours.

Because each day's swim workout time is no more than 30 minutes, many of the workouts have been adjusted accordingly. The instructions provided in the plan will help you focus each workout on the particular sets that are most important for sprint-distance racing. If the instruction directs you to reduce the sets by half, and the workout specifies four sets, you will swim just two. The distance of each interval is unchanged. Depending on your personal swimming speed, you may need to further modify the workouts if you want to keep your workout time near the 30-minute mark.

Best wishes for getting fast.

Note

If you are also using Gale's Training Plans for Multisport Athletes, *this plan is designed to dovetail with that book's "Faster Sprint-Distance Performance" program. If you are not following that particular plan for your triathlon training, you can still use the plan given here to provide structure for your swimming and help improve performance.*

Sprint-Distance Training Plan

Week	Time	Workout	TUESDAY Instruction	Time	Workout	THURSDAY Instruction	Weekly Total
1	0:30	E 4	After the warm-up, begin with the 100s.	0:30	E Form 3	Do half of the sets specified in the beginner workout.	1:00
2	0:30	30M 1	Use the workout appropriate for your current speed.	0:30	E Speed 1	Do half of the sets specified in the beginner workout.	1:00
3	0:30	Ta			Day off		0:30
4	0:30	30M 6	Do the beginner workout.	0:30	E Form 6	Do the advanced workout. Omit the 100s from the warm-up and do just 2 sets where sets are specified.	1:00
5	0:30	30M 4	Do the beginner workout.	0:30	E Speed 5	Only one time through the warm-up and main set. The 50s are the most important.	1:00
6	0:30	E 16	Use the beginner workout. Do only one set of the warm-up and begin with the second set of 4 × 100.		Day off		0:30
7	0:30	ME 7	Cut the warm-up by half and do half of the sets specified in the beginner workout.	0:30	E Form 3	Do half of the sets specified in the beginner workout.	1:00
8	0:30	30M 3	Do the beginner workout.	0:30	E Speed 1	Do half of the sets specified in the beginner workout.	1:00
9	0:30	Ta			Day off		0:30
10	0:30	ME 7	Cut the warm-up by half and swim just 2 sets of the 500 m and 300 m.	0:30	E Form 6	Do the advanced workout. Omit the 100s from the warm-up, and do just 2 sets where sets are specified.	1:00
11	0:30	AE 1	Do the beginner workout and eliminate the 300 K and 300 Easy.	0:30	E Speed 5	Do just one set of the warm-up and main set. The 50s are the most important.	1:00
12	0:30	ME 1	Go as far as you can through the main set until the clock hits 25 minutes. Cool down.		Day off		0:30
13	0:30	An 3	Eliminate all kicking and pulling in the warm-up.	0:30	OW 1		1:00
14	0:30	An 6	Reduce the warm-up and 100 sets to keep workout time to 30 minutes.	0:30	OW 2		1:00
15	0:20	E Speed 3	Warm up, do the 25s, cool down, and get out.			RACE (Sat. or Sun.)	0:20+

Note: Workouts may be done any day of the week. Days shown here are meant to demonstrate how best to space workouts over the course of a week.

Sprint

13-Week Olympic- and Half-Ironman-Distance Swim Plan

Because the swim distances in half-Ironman (1.2 miles) and Olympic races (0.9 miles) are similar, you can use this plan to prepare for either event. Depending on your swimming pace, select either the beginner or advanced workouts as a starting point. You may find that you need to modify them slightly to meet your personal needs.

If you are an experienced swimmer with solid speed in the water and you're pinched for training time, you can swim less than the plan suggests. In addition to eliminating the optional workout, reduce the Tuesday workout to just 30 or 45 minutes. Thursday and Saturday swims can be kept to 45 to 60 minutes. A final option is to swim only twice per week. If you are a good swimmer, your training time is best spent on the bike or running.

If you are using these workouts to supplement another plan, notice that the first 3 weeks of higher volume are followed by 1 week of rest, making up 4-week training blocks. The pattern changes in weeks 9 through 13 to allow for a peak and taper to race day. Repeat or adapt the pattern as needed.

Note

Before beginning this plan, you should know your current average pace per 100 for a distance of 1000 or 1500 meters or yards (see the Tb time trial).

If you are also using Gale's book Training Plans for Multisport Athletes, *this plan is designed to dovetail with the "13 Weeks to a Half-Ironman for Athletes with Limited Time" program. To combine the two, simply eliminate the optional Monday swim. Notice that some of the Tuesday Endurance swims are speed rather than form workouts. This change allows the Tuesday swim to include some faster swimming. If you get too tired, use the Endurance Form progression from the Ironman plan, but keep the training time lower, as shown in this plan.*

Drills to Improve Swimming Technique

Catch-up Drill

To do this freestyle drill, you will keep one arm in the forward position until the other arm completes a full stroke and reaches the forward position (i.e., "catches up"). If you start with your right arm forward, wait until the left arm completes a stroke and reaches the forward position again. Then complete a stroke with the right arm as the left arm remains in the forward position. Repeat for the designated distance.

Tip

Be sure to practice body rotation during freestyle drills, rolling your body toward the side of your working arm. Avoid keeping your body flat in the water, with your belly button pointing at the bottom of the pool, for the entire drill.

Fingertip Drill (FTIP)

This freestyle drill will help you remember to keep your elbows high on the recovery portion of your stroke. Simply drag your fingertips across the surface of the water.

Kicking Drill (K)

This drill isolates your kicking, whether you do it with or without a kickboard. Your arms should remain quiet, either streamlined along your body or out in front. If your arms are in front of your body, do not use a breaststroke pull, short or long, to take a breath. A slight press with locked hands will allow a quick breath.

If kicking without a kickboard, try to simulate normal swimming body position by pressing your chest toward the bottom of the pool, keeping the neck in a straight line with the spine. With your arms at your side, roll your body to the left or right for a breath.

Beginner: Place your hands in front, using a kickboard if you like. Lose the kickboard as you improve.

Intermediate: With your hands at your sides, roll to breathe on your preferred side.

Advanced: Keep your hands at your sides and practice breathing on your less dominant side.

Single-Arm Drill

Swim freestyle using just one arm for the designated length. To work the left arm (LT), keep the right arm at your side (beginners may position the right arm forward; see tips below); use a moderate kick and normal body position; and roll while the left arm performs a perfect stroke for the designated distance, typically 25 m. To work the right arm (RT), repeat the drill in the same way, keeping your left arm at your side. Beginners may use fins.

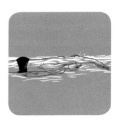 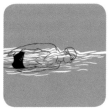 

Tips

Beginner: Do this drill with fins, with the resting arm in a forward position as if it were ready to begin a stroke cycle at any moment. Eliminate the fins as you improve.

Intermediate: Keep your resting arm at your side rather than extended to the front. You can use fins to keep your body position high in the water. Breathe on your right side.

Advanced: Eliminate the use of fins while keeping your left arm at your side. Then move your breathing to the left side.

Sculling Drill

Tips

Beginners may use fins for the sculling drills.

Front

In the prone position, stretch your arms out in front of you. Your hands will "scull" in a figure eight with fingertips pointing forward. To propel yourself forward, you will change pitch with your hands as you move them from side to side (a distance of roughly 6 to 8 inches), a simulation of the catch portion of your stroke. Your kick should be minimal, with the head up or down. Keep your hands within shoulder width.

Chest

In the prone position, bend your elbows and point your fingertips toward the bottom of the pool. Keeping your elbows high, do figure eights with your hands, using your hand and arm pitch for forward propulsion. This motion is similar to the center of the stroke.

Back

In the prone position, point your finger-tips toward your toes. Keeping your arms aligned with yur body, do figure eights to propel yourself forward. The sculling motion should not extend past shoulder width.

Supine Position

Floating on your back with hands at your sides and fingertips pointing toward your toes, move your hands in figure eights to propel yourself headfirst. Again, keep the sculling motion within shoulder width.

Underwater Recovery Drill (UW)

Keep your hands and arms underwater on the recovery portion of the stroke. Your head position will be the same as when swimming freestyle. This stroke is similar to a dog paddle, but your head remains down and you complete the entire propulsion phase all the way back. (In dog paddle, you shorten the back half of the stroke.)

Sighting Drill

The main purpose of lifting your head up while swimming is to catch a look forward in order to swim a straight line toward your destination. Before you do this drill, select something in the distance that is easily visible from the surface of the water. As you swim, take a normal breath to the side and then lift your head only enough to have  your goggles clear the surface of the water to take a look for your marker. You can do this immediately after taking the side breath or on the next stroke. Try to keep your stroke smooth and rhythmic; don't pause for the sighting phase. Keeping most of your face in the water prevents your hips from dropping too low, causing drag.

Glossary

B-3   Breathe every third stroke.

B-3,4,5   Breathe every third, fourth, and fifth stroke, designated by 25 m. For example:

6 × 75 B-3,4,5: Breathe every third stroke of the first 25 of the 75, every fourth stroke of the second 25, and every fifth stroke of the final 25.

Best average   Swim at the fastest average speed possible, achieving the best average time.

Build   Swim progressively faster within the designated set. A few examples:

25 Build: Gradually build speed throughout the 25 m, with the last 5 m being the fastest.
8 × 100 Build: Swim each length (25 m) within the 100 m faster than the last. Speed is built within the 100-m distance, meaning all eight 100s are to be swum at roughly the same speed.

Catch-up   A freestyle swimming drill in which one hand remains in the forward position until the other hand "catches up," or reaches the forward position. See "Drills to Improve Swimming Technique" for illustrated instruction.

Cooldown (C/D)   Aim to begin the cooldown in zone 2 and finish in zone 1.

Count   Count strokes per lap.

Descending (DESC)   With each swim interval, your time will incrementally decrease. For example:

8 × 100 DESC: Each 100-m interval is faster than the previous one. When the code reads DESC 2-2-2-2, you will swim every two sets at descending speed.

When the instructions read 8×100 DESC 2-2-2-2, the first two 100-m intervals are swum at a particular speed, the second two are faster, the third two are faster still, and the last two are the fastest swims of that set.

Distance per stroke (DPS) Maximize the distance that each arm can propel the body. Count the number of strokes per 25 m.

Drill (DR) Select any drill of your choosing. Examples are catch-up, fingertip drag, right arm, left arm, and sculling. See "Drills to Improve Swimming Technique" for illustrated instruction.

Easy Swim at zone 1 rating of perceived exertion.

Even/odd Instructions vary within a set according to even or odd repetitions. For example:

8 × 50 EVEN Build/ODD DPS: Build speed on repetitions 2, 4, 6, and 8. For repetitions 1, 3, 5, and 7, focus on distance per stroke.

Fast Swim as fast as you possibly can for the given distance. Your pace should vary depending on the distance—a fast 50-m swim will be faster than a fast 200-m swim.

Fingertip drill (FTIP) See "Drills to Improve Swimming Technique" for illustrated instruction.

Free/back Swim any combination of freestyle and backstroke.

Kick/strong kick Some workouts specify when or how hard to kick. In a longer race, triathletes typically conserve energy in the swim and limit their kick. When a workout calls for a harder kick, the purpose is to increase speed or fitness. These workouts are best used for conditioning, not tapering before a race.

Kicking drill (K)   See "Drills to Improve Swimming Technique" for illustrated instruction.

LT, RT (single-arm drill)   See "Drills to Improve Swimming Technique" for illustrated instruction.

Max speed   All-out fast, no holding back.

Moderate (MOD)   A moderate pace, zone 3 effort.

Negative split (N/S)   The second half of the designated swim is faster than the first half.

Perfect   Concentrate on good form: horizontal body position, a steady kick, and maximal distance per stroke.

Pull   Swim with pull buoys. Paddles are optional but should be used when working on force.

Race pace   The speed you intend to swim during the event. Race pace can be expressed as the average pace per 100 m for the event distance.

Repeat   Repeat the preceding set as specified. There is no extra rest between sets unless designated.

Rest interval (RI)   Many swim sets will have a designated rest interval. For example:

When a set is expressed as 3 × 100 SW 0:25RI, you would take a 25-second rest after each 100-m repetition. Here's another example: 200 (0:20RI) 300 (0:25RI) 200 (0:20RI). In this set, the swimmer would swim 200 m, rest 20 seconds, swim 300 m, rest 25 seconds, swim 200 m, rest 20 seconds, and then continue with the set. Once you begin rolling on the main set of the workout, try to take only the amount of rest designated on the workout. When there is no rest interval designated, you may rest as long as you please.

Glossary

Round   Special instructions may be given for each repeat swim set. For example:

If "Repeat 4 times" is instructed, round 1 may be swum at T-pace plus two seconds. The second time through the set, or round 2, may be swum at T-pace, round 3 at T-pace minus two seconds, and round 4 at T-pace minus five seconds.

Scull   See "Drills to Improve Swimming Technique" for illustrated instruction.

Single-arm drill (LT, RT)   See "Drills to Improve Swimming Technique" for illustrated instruction.

Swim interval (SI)   Designated swim intervals include both the swim time and the rest time. A swim interval may be designated by "T-pace + 0:20 SI." For example, assuming a T-pace of 1:20, 4 × 100 T-pace + 0:20 means you will swim 4 × 100 on a 1:40 interval. If you swim 100 m at a 1:20 pace, you will have 20 seconds to rest before beginning the next interval. Try to swim these sets at T-pace or slightly faster (i.e., by one to three seconds). The second way a swim interval may be designated is 1:00 SI, which means the swim and rest must be completed within a minute. For example 10×50 (1:00SI) means to swim 10 repeats of 50 m, leaving every sixty seconds.

T-pace   The pace you held in the time trial, T, for swimming. For example, if T-pace was 1:20 per 100 m, then T-pace for 200 is 2:40 and T-pace for 50 m is 0:40.

Underwater recovery   Hands and arms remain underwater on the recovery portion of the stroke. See "Drills to Improve Swimming Technique" for illustrated instruction.

Warm-up (W/U)   Gently increase speed throughout the warm-up.

Abbreviations

30M	30-minute workout
An	Anaerobic Endurance workout
B-3	breathe every third stroke
B-3,4,5	breathe every third, fourth, and fifth stroke
Back	backstroke
Best Avg	best average
C/D	cooldown
DESC	descending speed
DESC 2-2-2	descending speed every two sets
DPS	distance per stroke
DR	drill
E	Endurance workout
F	Force workout
Free	freestyle
FTIP	fingertip drill
K	kick
LT	left arm, single-arm drill
ME	Muscular Endurance workout
MOD	moderate, zone 3
N/S	negative split
OW	open-water workout
RI	rest interval
RT	right arm, single-arm drill

SI	swim interval
SW	swim any stroke
T (a or b)	test, time trial workout
T-pace	test pace
U/W	underwater recovery
W/U	warm-up

Test

W/U: 10–20 MINUTES, CHOICE

SPRINT-DISTANCE TRIATHLON

3 × 100   FAST   :20RI

The goal of the set is to swim at the highest possible sustained speed. Watch the clock and get your time on each 100. It is best if all three 100s are within five seconds of one another. Average the time for all three 100s to establish a T-pace.

C/D: CHOICE

Total Distance: 300+

W/U: 10-20 MINUTES, CHOICE

OLYMPIC- OR LONG-DISTANCE TRIATHLON

| 3 × 300 FAST | :30RI | The goal is to swim at the highest average speed possible. Watch the clock and get your time on each 300. All three 300s should be within fifteen seconds of each other. Average the time for all three 300s and divide the average by three to establish a T-pace for a 100-m distance. This particular pace is used to approximate lactate threshold pace. |

C/D: CHOICE

Total Distance: 900+

T

Endurance

W/U: 200 SW 2 × 200 (50 SW, 100 K, 50 SW) :20RI

BEGINNER

300, 200, 100	MOD	:20RI
200, 100, 50	N/S	:25RI
200	FAST	:30RI
100	FAST	:30RI
6 × 100	PULL	:25RI

C/D: 100

Total Distance: 2550

ADVANCED

400, 300, 200, 100	MOD	:20RI
300, 200, 100	N/S	:25RI
200	FAST	:30RI
100	FAST	:30RI
4 × 150	PULL	:20RI

Total Distance: 3200

E

1

Endurance

2

E

W/U: 6 × 75 DESC 2-2-2 :20RI

BEGINNER			ADVANCED		
2 × 200	DESC	:20RI	2 × 200	DESC	:20RI
100	MOD	:20RI	100	MOD	:20RI
2 × 200	DESC	:25RI	2 × 300	DESC	:30RI
100	MOD	:25RI	100	MOD	
2 × 300	DESC	:30RI	2 × 400	DESC	
100	MOD		100	MOD	:40RI

C/D: 6 × 75 (50 FREE, 25 BACK) :20RI

Total Distance: 2600   Total Distance: 3000

3

Endurance

W/U: 300 SW   200 K

BEGINNER		
4 × 200	150 SW, 50 K	:30RI
	1:00 bonus rest	
600	PULL N/S	1:00RI
16 × 25	DESC 2-2-2-2	:15RI

Total Distance: 2500

ADVANCED		
4 × 300	100 SW, 100 K,	
	100 SW	:30RI
	1:00 bonus rest	
600	PULL N/S	1:00RI
16 × 25	DESC 2-2-2-2	:15RI

Total Distance: 2900

C/D: 200 EASY

E

Endurance

W/U: 300 SW   300 K

BEGINNER			ADVANCED		
6 × 150	DESC 2-2-2	:20RI	8 × 150	DESC 2-2-2-2	:20RI
	1:00 bonus rest			1:00 bonus rest	
6 × 100	DESC 2-2-2	:15RI	8 × 100	DESC 2-2-2-2	:15RI
	1:00 bonus rest			1:00 bonus rest	
6 × 50	DESC 2-2-2	:10RI	8 × 50	DESC 2-2-2-2	:10RI

C/D: 100

Total Distance: 2500   Total Distance: 3100

E

Endurance

W/U: 300 SW   4 × 75 (25 K, 25 DR, 25 SW)   300 N/S BY 100

BEGINNER

4 × 100	T-PACE + :02 2:00–2:30SI
800	T-PACE
	Swim the first 100
	T-PACE and hold on
	2:00 bonus rest
6 × 100	DESC 2-2-2 2:00–2:30SI

ADVANCED

4 × 100	T-PACE + :02 1:45–2:00SI
800	T-PACE
	Swim the first 100
	T-PACE and hold on
	2:00 bonus rest
8 × 100	DESC 2-2-2-2 1:45–2:00SI

C/D: 6 × 50 FREE/BACK :20RI

Total Distance: 3000   **Total Distance: 3200**

E

Endurance

W/U: 3 × 300 (100 SW :30RI, 4 × 50 B-3 :20RI)

BEGINNER			ADVANCED		
3×			3×		
200	PULL	:20RI	200	PULL	:20RI
3 × 50	DESC 1–3 BY :01	:15RI	4 × 50	DESC 1–4 BY :01	:15RI
600	ODD EASY, EVEN 100s BUILD		800	ODD EASY, EVEN 100s BUILD	

C/D: 6 × 50 FREE/BACK :20RI

Total Distance: 2850

Total Distance: 3200

E

Endurance

W/U: 10-MIN. MIX

BEGINNER

2 × 400	N/S, *PULL Round 2*	:30RI
	1:00 bonus rest	
3 × 300	N/S, *PULL Round 3*	:30RI
	1:00 bonus rest	
3 × 200	N/S, *PULL Round 3*	:30RI
	1:00 bonus rest	
3 × 100	N/S, *PULL Round 3*	

Total Distance: 2700+

ADVANCED

3 × 400	N/S, *PULL Round 3*	:30RI
	1:00 bonus rest	
3 × 300	N/S, *PULL Round 3*	:30RI
	1:00 bonus rest	
3 × 200	N/S, *PULL Round 3*	:30RI
	1:00 bonus rest	
3 × 100	N/S, *PULL Round 3*	

Total Distance: 3100+

C/D: 100

15

E

Endurance

W/U: 2 × (200 SW, 200 PULL, 100 K)

BEGINNER		
12 × 25	DPS	:40SI
4 × 100	DESC 2-2	:20RI
4 × 75	PULL B-3,4,5	
	BY 25	:15RI
4 × 100	DESC 2-2	:15RI
4 × 75	PULL B-3	:25RI
2 × 100	FAST	:10RI

ADVANCED		
12 × 25	DPS	:40SI
6 × 100	DESC 2-2-2	:20RI
4 × 75	PULL B-3,4,5	
	BY 25	:15RI
4 × 100	DESC 2-2	:15RI
4 × 75	PULL B-3	:25RI
2 × 100	FAST	:10RI

C/D: 100

Total Distance: 3000

Total Distance: 3200

E

Endurance

W/U: 800 CHOICE

BEGINNER		
3 × 300	DESC 1-3	:40RI
100	K	
3 × 200	DESC 1-3	:30RI
100	K	
3 × 100	DESC 1-3	:20RI

ADVANCED		
3 × 300	DESC 1-3	:30RI
200	K	
3 × 200	DESC 1-3	:20RI
200	K	
3 × 100	DESC 1-3	:10RI

C/D: 100

Total Distance: 2900

Total Distance: 3100

E

18 Endurance

W/U: 200 SW   8 × 50 (25 CATCH-UP, 25 BUILD) :10RI

BEGINNER		
4 × 75	MOD	:15RI
4 × 50		:15RI
4 × 100		:20RI
200	EASY K	
3 × 200		:30RI
	2:00 bonus rest	
12 × 25	FAST	:40SI

ADVANCED		
6 × 75	MOD	:15RI
4 × 50		:15RI
4 × 100		:20RI
200	EASY K	
4 × 200		:30RI
	2:00 bonus rest	
12 × 25	FAST	:40SI

C/D: 200 (2 ROUNDS: 50 CATCH-UP, 50 BACK)

Total Distance: 2800   Total Distance: 3150

E

Endurance

W/U: 300 SW   200 K   6 × 75 (50 BUILD, 25 B-3) :15RI

E

BEGINNER

8 × 50	DESC 2-2-2-2	:15RI
4 × 75	K	:15RI
2×		
2 × 200	T-PACE	:20RI
	1:00 rest between rounds	
8 × 25	ODD BUILD, EVEN FAST	:45SI

Total Distance: 2850

ADVANCED

8 × 50	DESC 2-2-2-2	:15RI
4 × 75	K	:15RI
2×		
3 × 200	T-PACE	:20RI
	1:00 rest between rounds	
16 × 25	ODD BUILD, EVEN FAST	:35SI

Total Distance: 3450

C/D: 200 FREE/BACK

Endurance

W/U: 200 SW   100 K   200 SW

BEGINNER	
4 × 150	BUILD	:20RI
4 × 50	K	:15RI
4 × 100	BUILD	:15RI
4 × 75	K	:15RI
2 × 200	DESC	:30RI

ADVANCED	
4 × 150	BUILD	:20RI
4 × 50	K	:15RI
4 × 100	BUILD	:15RI
4 × 75	K	:15RI
4 × 200	DESC 2-2	:30RI

C/D: 200

E

Total Distance: 2600

Total Distance: 3000

1

Endurance Speed

W/U: 300 SW   200 K   100 SW   12 × 25 MOD   :10RI

BEGINNER

4×

| 200 | MOD | :20RI |
| 2 × 75 | FAST | :15RI |

:30 bonus rest

400   K (100 EASY, 200 MOD, 100 EASY)

ADVANCED

4×

| 300 | MOD | :20RI |
| 2 × 75 | FAST | :15RI |

:30 bonus rest

400   K (100 EASY, 200 MOD, 100 EASY)

C/D: 100

Total Distance: 2800

Total Distance: 3200

E speed

2

Endurance Speed

W/U: 10 × 50 :15RI 300 PULL

BEGINNER			ADVANCED		
300	T-PACE + :03	:20RI	400	T-PACE + :03	:20RI
3 × 100	T-PACE	:20RI	4 × 100	T-PACE	:20RI
200	T-PACE + :03	:20RI	300	T-PACE + :03	:20RI
2 × 100	T-PACE	:20RI	3 × 100	T-PACE	:20RI
100	T-PACE + :03	:20RI	200	T-PACE + :03	:20RI
100	UNDER T-PACE	:20RI	2 × 100	UNDER T-PACE	:20RI

C/D: 100 FREE/BACK

Total Distance: 2100   Total Distance: 2700

E speed

Endurance Speed

3

W/U: 400 SW   300 PULL   200 K

BEGINNER

5 × 150	T-PACE + :20	SI
200	N/S	:20RI
5 × 100	T-PACE + :10	SI
	2:00 bonus rest	
16 × 25	FAST/EASY, EASY/FAST,	1:00SI

ADVANCED

5 × 200	T-PACE + :20	SI
300	N/S	:20RI
5 × 100	T-PACE + :10	SI
	2:00 bonus rest	
16 × 25	FAST/EASY, EASY/FAST,	:40SI

C/D: 100

Total Distance: 2850

Total Distance: 3200

E speed

4

Endurance Speed

W/U: 300 SW   300 K   200 CATCH-UP

BEGINNER			ADVANCED		
4 × 200	ODD N/S	:15RI	4 × 300	ODD N/S	:15RI
2 × 200		:20RI	2 × 200		:20RI
200			300		
	2:00 bonus rest			2:00 bonus rest	
10 × 50			10 × 50		
2 rounds	1–4 BEST AVG	:45RI	2 rounds	1–4 BEST AVG	:45RI
	5 EASY			5 EASY	

C/D: 200

Total Distance: 2900   Total Distance: 3400

E speed

Endurance Form

1

W/U: 300 SW   300 K   300 PULL   200 SW   200 K   200 PULL

BEGINNER

3 × 50	RT/LT	:20RI
300	N/S	:30RI
3 × 50	FTIP	:20RI
300	N/S	:20RI
3 × 50	CATCH-UP	:20RI
2 × 300	N/S	:20RI

Total Distance: 3250

ADVANCED

4 × 50	RT/LT	:20RI
300	N/S	:30RI
4 × 50	FTIP	:20RI
300	N/S	:20RI
4 × 50	CATCH-UP	:20RI
2 × 300	N/S	:20RI

Total Distance: 3400

C/D: 100

E form

Endurance Form

W/U: 400 SW

BEGINNER		
8 × 50	25 RT/LT, 25 BUILD	:20RI
	1:00 bonus rest	
400	T-PACE + :06	:15RI
2 × 200	T-PACE + :02	:15RI
400	T-PACE + :05	:15RI
4 × 100	T-PACE	:15RI

ADVANCED		
8 × 50	25 RT/LT, 25 BUILD	:20RI
	1:00 bonus rest	
500	T-PACE + :06	:15RI
2 × 250	T-PACE + :02	:15RI
500	T-PACE + :05	:15RI
5 × 100	T-PACE	:15RI

C/D: 100

Total Distance: 2500

Total Distance: 2900

Endurance Form

W/U: 2 × 150 SW   100 K   50 DR

BEGINNER

4×

2 × 25	CATCH-UP	:10RI
2 × 25	UW RECOVERY	:10RI
4 × 25	BUILD	:15RI
2 × 600	N/S, DESC	:30RI

ADVANCED

4×

2 × 25	CATCH-UP	:10RI
2 × 25	UW RECOVERY	:10RI
4 × 25	BUILD	:15RI
2 × 800	N/S, DESC	:30RI

C/D: 100 FREE/BACK

Total Distance: 2550

Total Distance: 2950

E form

E

3

4

Endurance Form

E form

W/U: 300 SW   200 K   100 SW   200 K

BEGINNER		
3×		
200	PULL N/S	:30RI
3 × 100	DESC 1-3	:15RI
300	FREE, *EVEN 50s DPS*	

ADVANCED		
3×		
300	PULL N/S	:30RI
3 × 100	DESC 1-3	:15RI
300	FREE, *EVEN 50s DPS*	

C/D: 100

Total Distance: 2700

Total Distance: 3000

Endurance Form

W/U: 4 × 300 (100 SW, 100 K, 100 DRILL)

BEGINNER

8 × 50 ODD DPS,
EVEN BUILD 1:00SI

3×

150, 100, 50

Round 1 RI	:15, :10, :05
Round 2 RI	:20, :15, :10
Round 3 RI	:25, :20, :15

Total Distance: 2700

ADVANCED

12 × 50 ODD DPS,
EVEN BUILD 1:00SI

3×

150, 100, 50

Round 1 RI	:15, :10, :05
Round 2 RI	:20, :15, :10
Round 3 RI	:25, :20, :15

Total Distance: 2900

C/D: 200

E form

6 Endurance Form

E form

W/U: 150 SW 150 K 100 SW 100 K

BEGINNER

3 × 150	50 K	:10RI
	50 DPS	:10RI
	50 BUILD	:10RI
	2:00 bonus rest	
3 × 150	SW	:10RI
	300 50 K, 50 DPS	:30RI
2 × 150	SW	:10RI
	300 50K, 50 DPS	

ADVANCED

4 × 150	50 K	:10RI
	50 DPS	:10RI
	50 BUILD	:10RI
	2:00 bonus rest	
4 × 150	SW	:10RI
	300 50 K, 50 DPS	:30RI
3 × 150	SW	:10RI
	300 50K, 50 DPS	

C/D: 200

Total Distance: 2500   Total Distance: 2950

Force

W/U: 300 SW 200 K 100 SW 200 K 200 K

BEGINNER		
3×		
200	PULL N/S	:30RI
3 × 100	DESC 1-3	:15RI
300	K, *EVEN 50s FAST*	

ADVANCED		
3×		
300	PULL N/S	:30RI
3 × 100	DESC 1-3	:15RI
300	K, *EVEN 50s FAST*	

C/D: 100

Total Distance: 2700

Total Distance: 3000

3

F

4

Force

W/U: 10 × 50 :15RI 300 PULL

BEGINNER

6 × 100	PULL DESC 2-2-2	:20RI
400	SW B-3	
6 × 50	PULL DESC 2-2-2	:10RI
200	SW B-3	

ADVANCED

8 × 100	PULL DESC 2-2-2-2	:20RI
400	SW B-3	
8 × 50	PULL DESC 2-2-2-2	:10RI
200	SW B-3	

C/D: 200 FREE/BACK

Total Distance: 2500

Total Distance: 2800

F

Force

W/U: 200 SW 2 × 200 (50 SW, 100 K, 50 SW) :20RI

BEGINNER

3×

2 × 200	PULL	:20RI
4 × 50	PULL FAST	:30RI

1:00 bonus rest

4 × 50	SWIM W/ PADDLES	
	BEST AVG	1:15–1:30SI

Total Distance: 2700

ADVANCED

3×

2 × 200	PULL	:20RI
4 × 50	PULL FAST	:30RI

1:00 bonus rest

8 × 50	SWIM W/ PADDLES	
	BEST AVG	1:00SI

Total Distance: 2900

C/D: 100 FREE/BACK

F

5

Force

6

W/U: 300 SW   200 DPS   100 CATCH-UP

BEGINNER		
300	PULL	:30RI
3 × 100	SW	:10RI
300	PULL	:30RI
3 × 100	SWIM W/ PADDLES	:10RI
300	PULL	1:00RI
6 × 50	PULL FAST	:15RI

ADVANCED		
400	PULL	:30RI
3 × 100	SW	:10RI
400	PULL	:30RI
3 × 100	SWIM W/ PADDLES	:10RI
400	PULL	1:00RI
8 × 50	PULL FAST	:15RI

C/D: 200

Total Distance: 2600

Total Distance: 3000

F

Muscular Endurance

1

ME

W/U: 200 SW 200 K 200 PULL

BEGINNER

6 × 25	12.5 K, 12.5 SW	:15RI
5 × 100	T-PACE	:15RI
6 × 25	12.5 K, 12.5 SW	:20RI
5 × 100	T-PACE – :02	:15–:20RI
6 × 25	B-3	:25RI
5 × 100	T-PACE – :03	:15–:20RI

ADVANCED

6 × 25	12.5 K, 12.5 SW	:15RI
6 × 100	T-PACE	:15RI
6 × 25	12.5 K, 12.5 SW	:20RI
6 × 100	T-PACE – :02	:15–:20RI
6 × 25	B-3	:25RI
6 × 100	T-PACE – :03	:15–:20RI

C/D: 100

Total Distance: 2650

Total Distance: 2950

2

Muscular Endurance

W/U: 100 SW 300 (100 K, 100 DR, 100 SW) 6 × 50 BUILD :15RI

BEGINNER

4 × 100	T-PACE	:15RI
300	PULL	
3 × 100	T-PACE	:10RI
300	PULL	
3 × 100	T-PACE	:15RI

ADVANCED

8 × 100	T-PACE	:15RI
300	PULL	
4 × 100	T-PACE	:10RI
300	PULL	
4 × 100	T-PACE	:15RI

C/D: 100

Total Distance: 2400

Total Distance: 3000

ME

Muscular Endurance

W/U: 300 SW   300 K   200 CATCH-UP

BEGINNER

4 × 100	T-PACE – :01	:15RI
100	EASY	
3 × 100	T-PACE – :03	:15RI
100	EASY	
3 × 100	T-PACE – :05	:25RI
2 × 300	50 CATCH-UP, 25 RT, 25 LT, 50 PERFECT, 150 SW	:30RI

Total Distance: 2800

ADVANCED

6 × 100	T-PACE – :01	:15RI
100	EASY	
4 × 100	T-PACE – :03	:15RI
100	EASY	
4 × 100	T-PACE – :05	:25RI
2 × 300	50 CATCH-UP, 25 RT, 25 LT, 50 PERFECT, 150 SW	:30RI

Total Distance: 3200

C/D: 200

ME

9

Muscular Endurance

W/U: 4 × 175 (75 SW, 50 K, 50 BUILD DPS)

BEGINNER

4 × 150	100 BUILD,	:10RI
	50 FAST	:30RI
300	K	
4 × 100	75 BUILD,	:10RI
	25 FAST	:30RI
300	PULL	

Total Distance: 2500

ADVANCED

6 × 150	100 BUILD,	:10RI
	50 FAST	:30RI
300	K	
6 × 100	75 BUILD,	:10RI
	25 FAST	:30RI
300	PULL	:30RI

Total Distance: 3000

C/D: 200

ME

Muscular Endurance

W/U: 300 SW   300 K   300 CATCH-UP

BEGINNER

4 × 100	T-PACE – :01	:15RI
100	EASY	
3 × 100	T-PACE – :03	:15RI
100	EASY	
3 × 100	T-PACE – :04	:25RI
2 × 300		
4 rounds	RT, LT, CATCH-UP BY 25	

ADVANCED

6 × 100	T-PACE – :01	:15RI
100	EASY	
4 × 100	T-PACE – :03	:15RI
100	EASY	
4 × 100	T-PACE – :04	:25RI
2 × 300		
4 rounds	RT, LT, CATCH-UP BY 25	

C/D: 200

Total Distance: 2900

Total Distance: 3300

11

ME

Muscular Endurance

W/U: 200 SW   4 × 200 (25 RT, 25 LT, 150 BUILD)

BEGINNER		
14 × 75	T-PACE + :20	SI
1-4	T-PACE	
5-6	T-PACE - :02	
7-10	T-PACE	
11-12	T-PACE - :03	
13-14	T-PACE	

ADVANCED		
20 × 75	T-PACE + :20	SI
1-4	T-PACE	
5-8	T-PACE - :02	
9-12	T-PACE	
13-16	T-PACE - :03	
17-20	T-PACE	

C/D: 300 (3 ROUNDS: 50 CATCH-UP, 50 BACK)

Total Distance: 2350

Total Distance: 2800

ME

1 Muscular Endurance Distance

W/U: 300 SW   400 PULL   300 SW   200 K

MAIN SET

10 × 100 RACE PACE + :15	SI

Swim all 100s ± 1 sec.

Tip: *To add distance, take 1-2 min. rest after the main set, then repeat it.*

C/D: 300

Total Distance: 2500

ME distance

2 Muscular Endurance Distance

W/U: 200 SW   4 × 50 (25 SCULL, 25 SW)   4 × 75 BUILD

MAIN SET

| 4 × 200 | RACE PACE + :15
1:00 bonus rest | SI |
| 4 × 100 | RACE PACE + :15 | SI |

Swim each 100 2–5 sec. faster than race pace.

Tip: *To add distance, take 1–2 min. rest after the main set, then repeat it.*

C/D: 600 (3 ROUNDS: 100 SW, 100 K)

Total Distance: 2500

ME distance

3 | Muscular Endurance Distance

W/U: 400 SW   200 PULL   8 × 25 BUILD

MAIN SET

4 × 300	RACE PACE + :30 1:00 bonus rest	SI
6 × 50	RACE PACE + :30	SI Swim each 50 1-5 sec. faster than race pace.

Tip: To add distance, take 1–2 min. rest after the main set, then repeat it.

C/D: 300

Total Distance: 2600

ME distance

4 Muscular Endurance Distance

W/U: 200 SW   2 × 150 (50 K, 50 DR, 50 BUILD)

MAIN SET

2 × 400	RACE PACE + :30	SI
2 × 300	RACE PACE + :20	SI
4 × 100	RACE PACE + :30	SI

Desc 100s by 1–2 sec.

Tip: *To add distance, take 1–2 min. rest after the main set, then repeat it.*

C/D: 300

Total Distance: 2600

5 Muscular Endurance Distance

W/U: 4 × 150 (100 SW, 50 K NO BOARD) 200 DR

MAIN SET

2 × 500	RACE PACE + :30	SI
8 × 100	RACE PACE + :30	SI
8 × 50	RACE PACE + :20	SI

Desc 50s starting at race pace.

Tip: *To add distance, take 1-2 min. rest after the main set, then repeat it.*

C/D: 200

Total Distance: 3200

ME distance

Muscular Endurance Distance

W/U: 200 SW   5 × 100 DESC :30RI

MAIN SET

1000	RACE PACE + 1:30	SI
500		
5 rounds	75 EASY, 25 FAST	
	1:00 bonus rest	
10 × 100	RACE PACE + :30	SI

Desc 100s, starting at race pace.

Tip: *To add distance, take 1–2 min. rest after the main set, then repeat it.*

C/D: 300

Total Distance: 3500

ME

distance

7 Muscular Endurance Distance

W/U: 200 SW   6 × 50 (25 K, 25 DR)   300 PULL

MAIN SET

3 × 500	:30–1:00RI	On the 500s, sight every fourth 25.
3 × 200	:30RI	*Tip: To add distance, take 1–2 min. rest after the main set, then repeat it.*
6 × 50	RACE PACE + :10 SI	

C/D: 300

Total Distance: 3500

ME distance

Muscular Endurance Distance

W/U: 2 × 400 (100 SW, 100 K, 100 SW, 100 PULL)

MAIN SET

1500	2:00 bonus rest	On the 1500, sight every fourth 25.
5 × 200	RACE PACE + :30	SI	On the 200s, swim 50 FAST, 100 EASY, 50 MOD.

Tip: *To add distance, take 1-2 min. rest after the main set, then repeat it.*

C/D: 200

Total Distance: 3500

ME

distance

Muscular Endurance Distance

W/U: 300 SW   8 × 75 (25 K, 25 DR, 25 BUILD)   300 SW

MAIN SET

4 × 50	RACE PACE + :15	SI
	:30 bonus rest	
600		:30RI
	:30 bonus rest	
4 × 100	RACE PACE + :15	SI

On the 600, sight every third 25.

Tip: *To add distance, take 1-2 min. rest after the main set, then repeat it.*

C/D: 400

Total Distance: 2800

ME distance

W/U: 400 SW   200 K   400 PULL

MAIN SET

4 × 250
100 MOD, 50 BUILD, :30RI
100 MOD
1:00 bonus rest

Sight on 50 BUILD.
Swim second 250 10 sec. faster than first.

2 × 500   DESC   1:00RI

Tip: *To add distance, take 1-2 min. rest after the main set, then repeat it.*

C/D: 300

Total Distance: 3300

ME
distance

Anaerobic Endurance

W/U: 300 SW   8 × 75 PULL :15RI   300 K

BEGINNER

300	EASY	:30RI
3 × 75	FAST	:30RI
75	EASY	:20RI
2 × 75	FAST	:30RI
75	EASY	:20RI
75	FAST	:30RI

ADVANCED

500	EASY	:15RI
3 × 75	FAST	:30RI
75	EASY	:20RI
2 × 75	FAST	:30RI
75	EASY	:20RI
75	FAST	:30RI

C/D: 100

Total Distance: 2200

Total Distance: 2400

An

Anaerobic Endurance

W/U: 200 SW   4 × 50 (25 SCULL, 25 SW)   4 × 50 (25 K, 25 SW)

BEGINNER

4 × 100	FAST (75 SW, 25 K) :45RI
200	K WITH BOARD
	1:00 bonus rest

2×

| 5 × 50 | FAST | :30RI |
| | 2:00 rest between rounds | |

ADVANCED

6 × 100	FAST (75 SW, 25 K) 1:45SI
300	K WITH BOARD
	1:00 bonus rest

3×

| 5 × 50 | FAST | 1:00SI |
| | 2:00 rest between rounds | |

C/D: 200

Total Distance: 1900   Total Distance: 2450

An

3

Anaerobic Endurance

W/U: 300 SW 300 K 300 PULL 200 SW 200 K 200 PULL

BEGINNER

4 × 50	BUILD	:30RI
2 × 50	FAST	:30RI
50	EASY	:30RI
3 × 50	FAST	:30RI
50	EASY	:30RI
4 × 50	FAST	:30RI

ADVANCED

6 × 50	BUILD	1:00SI
4 × 50	FAST	1:00SI
50	EASY	1:00SI
6 × 50	FAST	1:00SI
2 × 50	EASY	1:00SI
4 × 50	FAST	1:00SI

C/D: 300 (EVERY THIRD 25 DPS)

Total Distance: 2550

Total Distance: 2950

An

4

Anaerobic Endurance

W/U: 2 × 400 (200 SW, 4 × 25 DPS :15RI)

BEGINNER

2×

2 × 75	SCULL/FTIP/ UW RECOVERY	:30RI
2 × 150	BUILD	:20RI
4 × 100	FAST	1:00RI
	2:00 rest between rounds	

300 SLOWER THAN T-PACE

ADVANCED

2×

2 × 75	SCULL/FTIP/ UW RECOVERY	:30RI
2 × 150	BUILD	:20RI
6 × 100	FAST	2:00SI
	2:00 rest between rounds	

500 SLOWER THAN T-PACE

C/D: 200 FREE/BACK

Total Distance: 2800

Total Distance: 3200

An

Anaerobic Endurance

5

W/u: 300 SW 300 K 300 PULL 200 SW 200 K 200 PULL

BEGINNER

4 × 75	FAST	:45RI
150	PULL	
3 × 50	FAST	:30RI
200	K	
3 × 50	FAST	:40RI

ADVANCED

6 × 75	FAST	2:00SI
300	PULL	
6 × 50	FAST	1:10SI
200	K	
6 × 50	FAST	1:30SI

C/D: 100

Total Distance: 2550   Total Distance: 3150

An

Anaerobic Endurance

W/U: 500 SW   18 × 25 (2 ROUNDS: 3 × 25 DPS, 3 × 25 COUNT, 3 × 25 BUILD) :10RI

BEGINNER		
6 × 100		1:00RI
	50 FAST	:10RI
	25 FAST	:05RI
	25 FAST	
4 × 50	DPS	:15RI
6 × 50	FAST	1:30RI

ADVANCED		
10 × 100		3:00SI
	50 FAST	:10RI
	25 FAST	:05RI
	25 FAST	
4 × 50	DPS	:15RI
6 × 50	FAST	1:30RI

C/D: 300

Total Distance: 2350

Total Distance: 2750

Anaerobic Endurance

W/U: 200 SW | 100 DRILL | 400 PULL

BEGINNER

3×

4 × 100   :40RI

1st 100	75 MOD, 25 FAST
2nd 100	50 MOD, 50 FAST
3rd 100	25 MOD, 75 FAST
4th 100	100 FAST

1:00 rest between rounds

300 PULL

Total Distance: 2300

ADVANCED

4×

4 × 100   1:45–2:30SI

1st 100	75 MOD, 25 FAST
2nd 100	50 MOD, 50 FAST
3rd 100	25 MOD, 75 FAST
4th 100	100 FAST

1:00 rest between rounds

300 PULL

Total Distance: 2700

C/D: 100

An

Anaerobic Endurance

W/U: 200 SW   100 K   8 × 50 (25 DRILL, 25 BUILD)

BEGINNER

2 × 250	50 BUILD, 100 EASY,
	100 BUILD :30RI
200	K NO BOARD
4 × 150	25 BUILD, 50 EASY,
	75 BUILD :20RI
200	K
4 × 100	FAST :45-1:00RI

ADVANCED

4 × 250	50 BUILD, 100 EASY,
	100 BUILD :30RI
200	K NO BOARD
4 × 150	25 BUILD, 50 EASY,
	75 BUILD :20RI
200	K
4 × 100	FAST 1:45-2:00SI

C/D: 100

Total Distance: 2700

Total Distance: 3200

An

30-Minute

W/U: 300 SW   4 × 50 (25 BUILD, 25 EASY) :10RI

BEGINNER

4 × 50	BUILD	:10RI
	1:00 bonus rest	
200	SW	:20RI
4 × 50	2-2-2	:10RI
	2:00 bonus rest	
3 × 100	T-PACE	:20RI

Total Distance: 1500

ADVANCED

6 × 50	BUILD	:10RI
	1:00 bonus rest	
300	SW	:20RI
6 × 50	2-2-2	:10RI
	2:00 bonus rest	
4 × 100	T-PACE	:20RI

Total Distance: 1900

C/D: 100

30M

1

30-Minute

W/U: 200 SW   3 × 100 (50 BUILD, 50 DPS) :15RI

BEGINNER

100	SW	:20RI
5 × 50	T-PACE	:15RI
100	SW	:20RI
3 × 50	FASTER THAN	:20RI
	T-PACE	
100	SW	
50	MAX EFFORT	:20RI

ADVANCED

200	SW	:30RI
5 × 50	T-PACE	:15RI
200	SW	:30RI
3 × 50	FASTER THAN	:20RI
	T-PACE	
200	SW	
2 × 50	MAX EFFORT	:20RI

C/D: 100

Total Distance: 1350

Total Distance: 1700

30M

30-Minute

W/U: 200 SW   4 × 50 (25 K, 25 BUILD) :15RI

BEGINNER

150	SW	:15RI
2 × 50	T-PACE	:15RI
50	SW	:15RI
4 × 50	T-PACE	:15RI
50	SW	:15RI
6 × 50	T-PACE	:15RI

ADVANCED

2 × 150	SW	:15RI
2 × 50	T-PACE	:15RI
2 × 100	SW	:15RI
4 × 50	T-PACE	:15RI
2 × 50	SW	:15RI
6 × 50	T-PACE	:15RI

C/D: 100

Total Distance: 1350

Total Distance: 1700

30M

3

30-Minute

4

30M

W/U: 100 SW   100 K   4 × 50 (25 BUILD, 25 CATCH-UP)

BEGINNER

100	PULL	:20RI
2 × 100	T-PACE + :02	:15RI
100	PULL	:20RI
2 × 100	T-PACE + :01	:15RI
100	PULL	:20RI
2 × 100	T-PACE	:15RI

ADVANCED

200	PULL	:20RI
2 × 100	T-PACE + :02	:15RI
200	PULL	:20RI
2 × 100	T-PACE + :01	:15RI
200	PULL	:20RI
2 × 100	T-PACE	:15RI

C/D: 200

Total Distance: 1500

Total Distance: 1800

30-Minute

5

W/U: 200 (2 ROUNDS: 50 DPS, 25 RT, 25 LT)   4 × 50 (25 FTIP, 25 DPS) :10RI

BEGINNER

2 × 50	BUILD	:15RI
200	T-PACE + :04	:30RI
2 × 50	BUILD	:15RI
200	T-PACE	:15RI
	1:00 bonus rest	
2 × 100	BEST AVG	1:00RI

ADVANCED

4 × 50	BUILD	:15RI
200	T-PACE + :04	:30RI
4 × 50	BUILD	:15RI
200	T-PACE	:30RI
	1:00 bonus rest	
3 × 100	BEST AVG	1:00RI

C/D: 200

Total Distance: 1400   Total Distance: 1700

30M

6

30-Minute

W/U: 300 (3 ROUNDS: 50 SW, 50 DR)

BEGINNER		
300	N/S	:30RI
200	N/S	:20RI
100	N/S	:15RI
50	N/S	:20RI
	1:00 bonus rest	
6 × 50	BEST AVG	:15RI

ADVANCED		
300	N/S	:20RI
200	N/S	:15RI
100	N/S	:10RI
200	N/S	:15RI
300	N/S	:20RI
	1:00 bonus rest	
6 × 50	BEST AVG	:15RI

Total Distance: 1350

C/D: 100

Total Distance: 1800

30M

Open-Water

W/U: 200 SIGHT 4 STROKES 200 SWIM TO SHORE :30RI

MAIN SET

200	BUILD
200	B-4 :30RI
200	15-STROKE BUILD
200	DPS
400	SIGHT 10 STROKES

Tip: *From your pool experience, you know how much time it takes to swim 200 at the given paces. Look ahead in the open water and estimate a distance of 200. Do your estimated distance and time coincide? Estimating distance and swim time in open water is a handy skill.*

C/D: STRETCH ON THE SHORE

Total Distance: 1600

1

Open-Water

W/U: 5 MIN. SIGHT 4 STROKES

MAIN SET

10 MIN.	T-PACE + :04
5 MIN.	SIGHT 6 STROKES
10 MIN.	6-BEAT KICK
5 MIN.	SIGHT 8 STROKES

Tip: When you increase the cadence of your kick to 6 beats per stroke cycle, try to minimize the vertical movement of your feet. Keep your heels submerged and think, "Motor-boat propeller, speed boost." Use this skill in shorter races or to help you accelerate past competitors.

C/D: 5 MIN. DPS
Estimated Time: 40 MIN.

Open-Water

W/U: 10 MIN. EASY

MAIN SET

4 ×

15 STROKES FAST AT PACE

15 STROKES CRUISE

10 MIN. CRUISE

Return to shore and

repeat set

Tip: *On the CRUISE portion, find the perfect stroke and pace combination to produce the most speed for the least energy cost. You will feel comfortable and relaxed at this speed, even though it is not "easy."*

C/D: RETURN TO SHORE

Estimated Time: 45 MIN.

OW

Open-Water

W/U: 5 MIN. EASY

MAIN SET

3×

20 STROKES	WITH KICK
20 STROKES	EASY
20 STROKES	BUILD
20 STROKES	WITH KICK

10 MIN. CRUISE

*Repeat main set as
you return to shore*

For the BUILD set, imagine you can see a slightly faster swimmer just ahead of you. Build your speed and add the kick to catch their draft. On the CRUISE portion, find the perfect stroke and pace combination to produce the most speed for the least energy cost.

Tip: *This workout is perfect for your taper. You can also use it to concentrate on your stroke or to do interval work in open water.*

C/D: STRETCH ON SHORE

Estimated Time: 35–50 MIN.

Open-Water

W/U: 10 MIN. B-4

5

MAIN SET

10 MIN.	T-PACE
5 MIN.	CRUISE WITH KICK
10 MIN.	INCREASE TEMPO
5 MIN.	CRUISE WITH KICK
	Return to shore
10 MIN.	INCREASE TEMPO
5 MIN.	CRUISE WITH KICK
10 MIN.	T-PACE

Sight every 8 strokes on the way out and every 10 on the way in. Experiment with lifting your head up to sight. Notice that the higher you lift your head, the more your hips dig in and drag. What is the least amount of head movement you can do to accomplish sighting, yet remain streamlined? Learn and practice this form for race day.

Tip: *This is a tough workout, great for Ironman-distance training. Do not attempt this workout during your taper.*

C/D: 10 MIN. EASY

Estimated Time: 70–90 MIN.

OW

Open-Water

W/U: 15 MIN. BUILD

MAIN SET

4x

20 STROKES	FAST TEMPO
20 STROKES	EASY WITH STRONG KICK
30 STROKES	FAST TEMPO
20 STROKES	CRUISE
5 STROKES	RECOVERY

Return to shore and repeat.

On the TEMPO and CRUISE sets, sight every 10 strokes.

Tip: *When you increase your tempo, try to swim fast. Anyone can swim "hard"; not everyone swims fast. Increase speed to drop your competition or people trying to draft on your heels.*

C/D: STRETCH ON SHORE

Estimated Time: 45 MIN.